It's a Bird!
¡Es un ave!

Elisa Peters

Traducción al español:
Eduardo Alamán

PowerKiDS & **Editorial Buenas Letras**™
press.   New York

For Jackie Patton

Published in 2009 by The Rosen Publishing Group, Inc.
29 East 21st Street, New York, NY 10010

First Edition

Editor: Amelie von Zumbusch
Book Design: Greg Tucker
Photo Researcher: Jessica Gerweck

Photo Credits: All images by Shutterstock.com.

Library of Congress Cataloging-in-Publication Data

Peters, Elisa.
  [It's a bird! Spanish & English]
  It's a bird! =¡Es un ave! / Elisa Peters ; traducción al español, Eduardo Alamán. – 1st ed.
    p. cm. – (Everyday wonders = Maravillas de todos los días)
  Added t.p. title: Es un ave!
  Includes index.
  ISBN 978-1-4358-2526-0 (library binding)
  I. Title. II. Title: ¡Es un ave!
  QL676.2.P4618 2009
  598–dc22
                                                2008006801

Manufactured in the United States of America

Web Sites: Due to the changing nature of Internet links, PowerKids Press and Editorial Buenas Letras have developed an online list of Web sites related to the subject of this book. This site is updated regularly. Please use this link to access the list:
www.powerkidslinks.com/wonder/bird/

Contents/Contenido

Birds are covered in **feathers**.

Las aves están cubiertas
de **plumas**.

Every bird has two wings
and a **beak**.

Las aves tienen dos alas
y un **pico**.

Birds come in many different shapes, sizes, and colors.

Hay aves de muchos formas, colores y tamaños.

9

Some birds, like this **rainbow lorikeet**, are very colorful.

Algunas aves, como este **loro australiano**, tienen muchos colores.

Many birds eat seeds.

Muchas aves comen semillas.

Other birds eat berries.

Otras aves comen bayas.

Seabirds, like this **puffin**,
most often eat fish.

Las aves marinas, como este
frailecillo, comen pescado.

Mother birds lay eggs in a nest.

Las aves mamá ponen sus huevos en nidos.

In time, baby birds break
out of these eggs.

Con el tiempo, las aves bebé
salen de sus huevos.

Mother birds take good
care of their babies.

Las mamá ave cuidan muy
bien a sus bebés.

Words to Know/Palabras que debes saber

beak
(el) pico

feathers
(las) plumas

puffin
frailecillo

rainbow lorikeet
loro australiano

Index

Índice